Love, the Monster in the Closet

By

Asher Faun

©2023 by Asher Faun
Flashpoint Publications
First edition July, 2023

FLASHPOINT
PUBLICATIONS

ISBN 978-1-61929-523-0

Cover Design by AcornGraphics

Publisher's Note:

Dedication

*For the little kid
who didn't think they'd
make it out alive.*

We did it.

Epigraph

Hello

You don't have to be afraid

I'm only telling the truth

On second thought

Maybe you should run

Table of Contents

Bleeding Eyes Trembling Hands

Broken Knuckles Splinted Bones

Hopeful Souls Hallowed Bodies

BLEEDING EYES
TREMBLING HANDS

ODE TO THE WORDS I NEVER WROTE

The poem I will never start

The poem I will never finish

The words spilled out

Wiped up, rewritten

Deleted and forgotten

Tip of my tongue

Never ending river

Never ending flood

Creating

Destroying

Never enough

Always too much

The flood

And the drought

Always unfinished

THE UNHEARD PRAYER

Midnight strikes

And all I can ask is

God, forgive me

Trembling lips whisper prayers

Shaking hands clasp tightly

I can feel my prayer

Fly through the walls

Take a turn in the clouds

Nosedive with frozen wings

And land on your doorstep

It curls into itself and shivers

I feel it die unheard

ON LOSS

You were always there

A constant companion

My closest friend

I'm so sorry

It was getting too bad

You were nearing the end

My closest friend

I'm so sorry

The ground was cold

The air was cold

You were cold

We buried you beneath

A blanket of stars

To guide you

I cannot see the stars

They went with you

The moon remains

She always does

But I do not know the way

Without you, I'm lost

My closest friend

I'm so sorry

GOODBYE

You left

And I am still here

I do not blame you

They dig, again

Again, I am small

The dirt pile grows

And I shrink

We've been here before

It doesn't get easier

9-1-1

Am I still breathing?

Lungs deflated

Inflated

Punctured

Puncture wounds

Stitched shut

Still bleeding

I can't breathe

My blood or hers?

Call an ambulance

Call a hearse

LITTLE MORE (THAN NOTHING)

I'm losing my mind

And you blame it on me

But is it truly my fault?

When I hear what they say

How far ahead of me they are

That colleges want well-rounded

Robots who are in a million clubs

That play sports and get top grades

All screws and bolts and motor oil

But I am not that

Because I think and I feel and I *bleed*

I bleed all the reasons I'm not good enough

I bleed all the reasons I don't love myself

I bleed all the reasons I won't make it in the world

And I lose my mind a little more

A little more

Blame it on me

A little more

Hate myself

A little more

Break my mind

A little more

Bleed

A little more

MY NAME

Office supplies

Turned into art

Paperclip smiles

Push-pin buttons

Sticky-note clothing

What is my name?

Just another file

A shuffled paper

I could not sit still

You tied me down

What is my name?

Stapled my feet

To the ground beneath

This monster

That you call a desk

You took my dream

Dipped it in ink

Now a paperweight

What is my name?

The smile carved

Into my cheeks

Ignoring my tears

Throat singed with coffee

Burns to speak

I do not speak

What is my name?

I am manufactured

Mass produced

Strings attached

Face pained on

What is my name?

Just another carbon copy

Just another file

ROBOTS

Pale faces

Dead eyes

Illuminated by harsh lights

Muted colors

Staggered steps

Everyone is always the same

"I'm different"

And yet

The mold is left unbroken

YOUTH

Little child,
Dreaming of dragons
Wishing for adventure
Choose your battles
Before they choose you

Oh, the gold
They didn't tell you
That it was cursed

"You have too much
Talent / brainpower / etc.
To let it go to waste"
I'm sorry,
I didn't know
That I was obligated
To be extraordinary

Little child,
Don't you know
That you never
Had a choice

Little child,

Don't you know

That you never

Had a chance

WARNING LABELS

They didn't tell me

How much it would hurt

Oh, how I needed a warning

To love someone

To build courage to tell them

To fail so spectacularly

We were not art

It was not beautiful nor poetic

It was just painful

STICKERS

The finality of stickers

Is a hard-learned lesson as a child

But one that lasts a lifetime

The disappointment when you realize

That you've placed it in the wrong spot

And that once removed

It will never work the same

When I realized that once put up

They were stuck there for good

I stopped putting stickers up

I was afraid I'd mess them up

And when I got older

They wondered

Why I had commitment issues

NIGHTMARE I – OPEN WOUNDS

Sometimes I wonder

If you think I'm lying

Or if you think I do it

Just for attention

I'm so tired

Always on the verge

Of falling asleep

Always on the verge

Of falling away

Can you feel it

When I wake up?

The hollow-point pain

Phantoms of ghosts of whispers

Screaming for an end to my sanity

Gnawing at what once was

Mauling what will be

I look in the mirror

And wonder where I went

ON SPECULATION

Let's talk about why I don't sleep

Maybe it's the way the screams
Seem to resound off the walls
Of the prison cell that is my mind
Even while I am wide awake

Maybe it's all that red
Coating the walls, the floor, the knife
Baptizing me in an ocean of sorrow
As I try desperately not to drown

Maybe it's the air squeezing from my lungs
As I claw at my throat begging for air
While the noose tightens, the water deepens,
And I learn what it feels like to die

Maybe I have insomnia
Maybe I'm just scared
Of what I might see

A I R

I can't breathe

I can't breathe

This is what it feels like

To drown without water

I can't breathe

I can't breathe

My mind is spinning

My chest is tight

I can't breathe

I can't breathe

My vision is fading

With eyes wide open

I can't breathe

I can't breathe

Don't tell me it's in my head

I already know that

I can't breathe

I can't breathe

You want to help

But don't know how

But don't know why

I can't breathe

I can't breathe

I can't breathe

I can't breathe

And you don't know how to help

CHOREOGRAPHY

I never should have told you

I never should have let you in

I can see you watching

Watching

Watching

You can see me breaking

Breaking

Breaking

S t o p

Don't let me fall

I can't trust you

S t o p

Pull on my strings

Watch me dance

S t o p

I know the steps

I know the lyrics

S t o p

I know the lies

I know the lies

I know the lies

Just make it stop

DEJA VU

In kindergarten I stood tall
Dressed in a pink dress
And my favorite shoes
In front of the whole class
So excited to give the daily announcements

You picked up my skirt
The teacher did nothing
I stopped wearing that dress
I didn't give the announcements again

In eighth grade we met again
After I'd forgotten who you were
And I thought you were nice
I really did like you
I thought we could have a future together

You stopped talking to me
Stopped putting in effort
Started talking to someone else
Started loving someone else
I'd forgotten who you are

TONGUE TWISTER

I'll shut up

I'll shut up

I should stop talking

Stop

Stop

Stop

Stop Talking

Chit chat

Chit chat

Shut up

Shut up

Shut up

Cut out my tongue

I don't want it anymore

MIDNIGHT WONDERINGS

Some nights I wonder

How the stars continue burning

With nothing to feed them

Other nights I am reminded

That I, too, drown myself in flame

Just to prove that I exist

I wonder if the ancient gods

Born of fire and ash

Are reduced to what they came from

I wonder if they watch us

And if they regret

Ever touching fire

Ever making us

OPEN PRAYER

Shaking hands

Clasped in prayer

"Oh god,

I want to change"

Sinning lips

Sinning hands

Soot-black soul

"Was I ever

Truly clean?"

I won't ask

For forgiveness

That train left

Long ago

There was an angel

Who loved you so much,

He couldn't bring himself

To love humanity

Long ago

You cast him out

Long ago

I gave up on humanity

Long ago

I waited for an answer.

"Have you cast me out?"

How long ago?

ON MEDUSA

Mother do you still love me?

My sweet child

How I cried

When the gods forsook you

I will always love you

COUSIN

The closest thing to a family reunion
That my family is willing to have
Happens to be a funeral

I'm marched around the funeral home
Donning my best Sunday dress
And trying to ignore the smell
Of the dead man at the front of the room
As I meet my obscure relatives

I'm brought before an old woman
Wrinkles like caverns lining her face
And my face reflects in her watery eyes
While I morbidly wonder if she's next
To occupy the dreaded box in front

Everyone I meet is introduced
As yet another cousin
The man in the coffin? Cousin
The old woman? Cousin
The children? Cousins

Their parents? Cousins

I learn that my family runs

To the ends of the universe

I can look up at a sky filled with stars

And call them my cousins

TO [REDACTED], WHAT I COULDN'T SAY

It's worse than you think. She did hit me. She's always hit me. I need help. I need to get out of this house, away from her, but I'm too scared. I'm too fucking scared. I'm in so much pain. Everything hurts all the time. Yes, I want your help. I've needed help for so long. I need to go to the hospital. If not for the severe depression, then for the anxiety, or the bulimia, or the self-harm, or even just to get me the fuck away from her.

Three days ago she was screaming at me again.

Three weeks ago she hit me in the throat.

Three months ago she was going through my stuff.

Three years ago she threatened me with a knife.

Yes, I need your help.

ODE TO EMPTY HALLS

Oh, you empty skeleton of buildings

Oh, you forgotten fossils and bare bones

Where the heartbeat of steps once flowed

Like a river unending and unstopping

What is your beauty?

The run-down look of your floors

A testimony to wandering souls

The graffiti on your walls

The finest art without a display case

The pin-drop silence

Loud and bold and suffocating

Oh, you wondrous mystery

Oh, you keeper of the unknown

What is your beauty?

BROKEN KNUCKLES

SPLINTERED BONES

LAMENT OF THE FALLEN

A ball of rage

Sits in my stomach

I will not speak your name

A web of sadness

Stretches across my mind

I still don't quite know why

A longing ache

Weighs down my soul

Arthritis in my wings

A hollow call

Escapes my lips

The song is bittersweet

OUT OF THAT HELLISH NIGHT

I can feel the eyes on me

Watching, waiting patiently

For me slip up, to fall

Grinning teeth

Smiling fangs

The vultures circle

They're waiting for me

They can't wait for my corpse

For my blood to be spilled

To tear the flesh from my bone

I won't face my fate afraid

I look them in the eyes

Grinning teeth

Smiling fangs

Dripping blood

Mine or theirs?

We'll have to wait

For one of us to drop

Before either one finds out

We circle each other

Grinning teeth

Smiling fangs

Dripping blood

I refuse to die quietly

I refuse to let my rage go

I refuse to let you win

Not like this

Not ever like this

Grinning teeth

Smiling fangs

Dripping blood

I refuse to die quietly

I refuse to die at all

THEY SHOULD HAVE WARNED YOU ABOUT ME

One time I said my smile

Was just me baring my teeth

And was no different from

The snarling fangs of an animal

I stand by the warning

That you should not trust me

I stand by the warning

That you should not trust

That trust leads to pain

I still haven't learned

From my past mistakes

But neither have you

I stand by the idea

That the stars are just angels

And shooting stars

Are them coming to visit us

And that things don't always

Go as they're planned

I stand by the fact

That everyone we love

Will one day leave us

And that love can only

End in sadness

I stand by the idea

That there are angels

Who broke their halos

And joined us mortals

I stand by the idea

That some demons

Stayed here too

I am not an angel

I am no demon

And yet I warn you

Do not trust me

I stand by the idea

That forgiveness is optional

That we are allowed to be

Angry and bitter

And I've been hurt

Again and again

Again and again

And I get back up

And I rarely forgive

"JUSTICE FOR ALL"

I'm screaming

For every injustice

That we've faced

She tells me

To let it go

He tells me

To let it go

But I am neither

He nor she

And I will not let it go

I'm fighting

For every injustice

That we've faced

And I'm going for blood

APOLOGIES

Tired and I don't know why

Angry but my voice is already hoarse

From screaming while happy

I refuse to apologize

I won't explain my actions

I'm trying to protect you

Paint me a demon, I don't care

No one can tell me

What my scars are from

White noise, white walls

Black hands, black heart

My soul is permanently stained

I'm trying to do what's right

You didn't give me a choice

Then told me I chose wrong

EDITS

Fix me

Fix my face

Fix my looks

But my tongue is still untamed

Break me

String me up

Dancing puppet

But my tongue is still untamed

Correct me

Fix my mannerisms

Fix my behavior

Cut out my tongue

Watch the words spill out anyways

HOMOSAPIENS OF THE CONCRETE JUNGLE

12pt font, Times New Roman

Click clack click clack

The classroom always smells

Like lost hope and decay

Post-it notes and paperclips

Are all that hold us together anymore

The assembly line shuffles on

Somehow stand-still traffic never stops

Eyes stare downward, everyone is busy

Too busy to talk/think/breathe/live

Yet laughter screams through the hallway

I wonder if the walls themselves mock us

Teachers stalk up and down

An endless sea of desks

We swim through assignments

While they taste the water for blood

ERROR

Empty

Empty, not full

Never enough

Never empty

Hollow out my ribcage

Hollow out my bones

Hollow out my flesh

Delete me from existence

Brain like an overloaded memory card

Deleting my memories

One by one

By ones and zeros

Zeros are empty

I just want to be empty

Too much

Too full

My brain overloads

Ones and Zeros

Error: Delete

ON LEADING

"I'm staying here
Or I'm leaving"
My smile doesn't falter
When he points to the door
Expecting me to back down
But I am stubborn today
And I spin around
And leave

"He said he likes
Your confidence but not
Your decision making"
I laugh when she asks
If we're going back in
And keep doing my work

"You're supposed
To be a leader"
That's bullshit
I'm not a leader
Not a good example

I am what you tell kids

Not to grow up to be

My rebel soul

Thrives in chaos

While feigning order

I'm always tired

I'm always angry

I'm bitter and mean

And I don't like people

Do not expect me

To be a leader

Or I will lead you

Straight to ruin

THE DAY SCHOOL WAS MORE IMPORTANT THAN OUR LIVES

The year there was a school shooting threat

And the morning that it was to happen

The police announced that they'd apprehended

A suspect

Nothing was confirmed

I was sent off to school anyways

                    Stare into the cavernous mouth

                    Of the high school entrance doors

                    As they swallow soul after hollow soul

                    And wondering why your own feet

                    Continue to shuffle forward

By second period rumors have spread

That the shooter wasn't working alone

So I called my mother for answers

But *a* suspect was apprehended

So it must have been safe now

I texted my friend to be careful anyways

Staff remind you that they are willing

To lay down their lives to protect you

And then send you into the hallways

Herded like cattle for slaughter

Who is the wolf in sheep's clothing?

By the end of the day we are calmer

We haven't learned anything in classes

But at least we are no longer crying

Not because *a* suspect is confirmed

But because we all made it

Because we are still alive

And that's all that matters

Do you feel safe?

I FIGHT

The last time

A drop of my blood

Parted with me

I could almost feel

My body fighting

Just to keep me alive

After just losing

Just a single drop

Just a single drop

But still my body

Fights just the same

And I know now

The only difference

Between a drop

And a gallon

Is how hard

I must fight

And I know now

The only difference

Between living

And dying

Is how hard

I fight

And so the battle rages on

And I fight

FIRE

The rebel's scream

The Bloody knuckles

Splattered paint

And raw emotion

The pulsing blood

The love and lust

Matchstick strike

Every flame

Every blaze

The adrenaline rush

The freedom in breathing

That fire in your lungs

I have no wings

Try to convince me

That I am not a dragon

I will turn you to ash

As I agree with you

Don't come too close

You'll burn with me

This is my fire

My passion

My paint

They ask

Does it scare me?

They don't understand

The beauty I see

They just hear the cry

Don't step too close

To the fire

RIPTIDE

I've always been partial to water sports

Chlorine was the scent of my childhood

And I learned how to swim

Before I touched the handlebars of a bike

My father has always been a runner

Not for sport, of course, but from us

He ran from his responsibilities

Ran from his family

Ran from his children

Ran from me

I live only in two extremes:

Drought or drowning

My mother taught me to swim

My father left me to die

I would say that he can burn

As penance for his sins

But in all honesty,

I would rather he drown

HERE BEFORE

Shadows dancing on the wall

Flicker of a new flame

Shadows dancing on the wall

World will never be the same

Raging fire, burning all

World will never be the same

Mass destruction, hollow call

Bloody knuckles, rebels tame

Mass destruction, hollow call

The story is still the same

First comes madness, then the fall

The story is still the same

Break the pattern, burn the lie

We've been here before

Break the pattern, burn the lie

We've been here before

LOOKING BACK

I'm trying to believe, but

When they said you were real

I could see through the lie into your hollow soul

I've only ever known

What if feels like

To love with everything I have

The feeling of fighting

To protect who you love

Is more strengthening than love itself

A hopeless battle

Rallies dreamers under a lie

But when I call on the truth they hide

I'm trying to believe, but

I've only ever known

The feeling of fighting

A hopeless battle

ON MY FAITH

Yaweh, Jehovah

They call his name

Without truly knowing it

They condemn me

Condemn mine

"In the beginning"

But there is no beginning

"Amen."

But there is no end

Miracle miracle

Burn the witch

Tell me our differences

And in the flames

I'll pray for you

REBEL SOUL

We glorify the rebel soul
And ridicule the rebel act

How dare you write about
My bloody hands and then
Scoff at how they got that way

Call me a failure
And I'll show you
What terrorizes kids
Hiding in dark corners

There is a time for fighting
But I don't remember when
This battle even began

"You should choose your battles"
But I never even had a choice

THE LAST DAYS

If I set the world on fire

Would you laugh or cry?

And if I couldn't sleep tonight

Would you sing a lullaby?

//

The windows are all broken

The stars have all gone out

Heaven shut its gates

Hell's run out of room

The angels burned their halos

And even the devil is scared

//

No rest for the wicked

None for the good either

I suppose those in between

Just have to wait and see

//

But the pyros are still thriving

Matchstick kids run the streets

And ragtag families drink gasoline

//

The militia strung up their boots

And that man hanging from the tree

They make the laws around here

They said he was corrupt

And had horns on his head

I think he called it a crown

But his silver tongue muddled the words

//

The sunset is still bloody and red

As the horizon swallows it whole

I wonder if it was once a planet

I wonder if it looked like ours

I wonder who lit that match

HOPEFUL SOULS

HALLOWED BODIES

LESSONS

As the youngest sibling,

I was always given the broken controller

When playing video games with my brothers

And it taught me a few life lessons

1. When the world tries it hardest

To push you in every wrong direction

Push back with equal force

Or you might find yourself at a cliff's edge

2. When you stop moving forward

It's usually a clear sign

That something in your life

Needs to be shaken up

3. Don't let your siblings give you

A controller that doesn't work

And when they do anyways

Definitely don't let them win the game

HOME

Home is where the heart is
Home is laughter around a table
Smiles so wide that they hurt
Laughs so hard that they ache

Home is listening intently
As my brothers tell stories
Of their own lives' adventures
And hearing my mother sigh
As she sets food on the table
And gives in to laughter with us

Home is "let me show you this picture"
And "how is your cat doing?"
It's "can you make this for my party?"
And "stop touching my hair"
It's everything being different
And nothing having changed at all

SURVIVORS

My love and I

The dogs stepping about our feet

The cat watching from afar

Songs play from our past

Pain and sentiment intertwined

As we eat without worry

I bounce in my seat

She calls me goofy

And I sneak the pups some dinner

When she offers to wash the dishes

My body does not remember the panic

I do not feel the guilt

Or maybe I do

But I am safe now

I am not in trouble

We spend the rest of the night reminiscing

We text old friends and watch familiar shows

Our scars pull but we laugh despite them

We are not the products of our past

Merely the survivors of them

YOU

I remember now

Why I fell so hard

Why it hurt so much

Why I risked it all

It was you

It was all you

SWEET

Oh, sweet honey

Drips from your words

Eyes like the sea

Voice like the echo

Of a long past ancient god

Sweetheart, do you bleed gold?

I suppose that's what

You want to know too

My hands in yours

You ask me how I stay

But I can't tell

If I'm addicted

Or just praying

Oh, sweet honey

Pours from my fingertips

Bleeds gold into pages

Drips from my papers

Drips from my lips

Drips from yours

IRONY

What's funny

Is that I've never

Loved someone

As much as I do you

I've never wanted

Someone to stay

As much as I do you

And yet

I've never wanted

To push someone away

As much as I do you

Oh, sweet irony

To love someone enough

To crave their hatred

And to want them to stay

All the while

MIDNIGHT

It is midnight

When I know

What I'd known for a while

But it was midnight

When the realization

Hits me in the chest

And reverberates in my heart

Like the sound of fireworks

It does not know

What a resting heart rate is

It is midnight

When I know

I would follow you

To the depths of hell

If it meant I could stay

By your side for forever

It is midnight

When I know

That my worst fear

Is not death

Is not torture

Is not losing myself

That it is losing you

Because that pain

Would be unbearable

It is midnight

When I know

That you care too

Maybe not the same way,

But at least you care

It is midnight

When I know

I love you

Midnight has passed

And I know

You love me too

SPARE HER I

I don't care

What I must go through

If only it would spare her

From feeling this pain

I would take a thousand arrows

I would walk through fire

And freeze to death

If it would save her

War is nothing

I'd spill oceans of crimson

I'd bleed out the sun

If it spared her

SPARE HER II – SPARE YOU

Panic attacks

Compressed lungs

Oceans of tears

To keep you here

Siphon the air

Fresh from my lungs

Flesh from my bones

Blood from my veins

To keep you here

I'd give you the world

I'd burn it for you

If it would spare you

If that's what it took

To keep you here

SPARE HER III – GOODBYE

I fight so hard

To keep you here

With no intention

Of keeping you

You deserve to live

You deserve to thrive

I will fight for you

But I cannot stay

I will not stay here

I cannot stay here

I can't do that

Not to you

SPARE HER IV – DON'T GO

You don't get to say goodbye
That's always been my line

Last time someone abandoned me
I swore I'd never beg for someone
To stay with me never ever again
But all I can think now is
"God, if you are listening
Please don't take her from me."

God, if you are listening
Please don't leave me

SPARE HER V – STAY

When I wake up

From a nightmare

Where I hurt you

I panic

My head tells me not to stay

My head tells me you won't want me

My head tells me I hurt you

You tell me otherwise

You tell me to stay

And I want to

My heart wants me to stay

And how could I say no to you?

SEMICOLON

My friend comes to school

With a semicolon tattooed on his arm

;;;

I ask him why and he rolls his sleeve up further

To show me scars, faded, but familiar

;;;

He tells me that a semicolon means

That the sentence was meant to end

But continued on anyway

;;;

He rolls his sleeve back down

Without need for further explanation

;;;

I know what he means;

I, too, stood at the cliff's edge;

I, too, lived another day

OPEN // CLOSED

Open
Open hands
Open hearts
Open with me
I am not good at open

Closed
Close my mouth
Close my eyes
Close myself off
I am *very* good at staying closed

Meet me halfway
Tell me half of your secrets
And I'll divulge half of my own
We can fill in the gaps
Just like we do with our hearts
Cracked and flawed
Scarred beyond recognition
Fearful beyond belief
I can hold your hopes/dreams/fears/regrets
As long as you hold mine too

AN OPEN LETTER TO MY SHADOW

A push and a pull

My light self and darkness

Tell me, lover,

Why do you look back at me

So disappointed

Dissatisfied

Distant

In this mirror?

We'll try again tomorrow

OK

I will be ok one day

I swear it

I swear it by the moon

I swear it by the air in my lungs

I swear it by the blood in my veins

I swear it by the blood in hers

We will be ok

I swear it

HER

She burned like the sun

And he was held hostage by her beauty

Looking at her in fleeing glances

Eyes burning each time he did

Never quite seeing all of her at once

Afraid he'd go blind if he did

Never quite able to look away long

Afraid he'd go blind if he did

She begged him to stay away

Warned him of the dangers of loving her

Warned him of the dangers of her love

And when he finally touched her,

Skin turned to coal-black ash

As the fire spread from his heart

To his skin and burned him whole

Their tears singed away in the heat

As he burned before her

HIM

His tears mixed with wax
Burning his skin
The burden on his back
Was finally lifted

It's funny how
When he was falling
He felt lighter
Than when he flew

They said she was his downfall
But when he got close enough
He asked her to free him
And she only complied

Fire kissed his skin
And freed him of the sky
She caught him in the waves
And cooled his blessed scars

She was his beloved savior

From the curse on his back

She was his saving grace

They just couldn't see how

NICKNAMES

They laughed

When they gave us

Our nicknames

"Cap and Bucky"

They didn't realize

How right they were

Neither of us

Are stable

And yet

We keep each other going

"If you go, I go"

Doesn't that sound like

"I'm with you

'Til the end of the line"?

If I'm honest

I already fell for you

If I'm honest

I could go through hell

And you'd still be the one

Who brings me back

If I'm honest

Yours would be the last name

I ever spoke

COLD

Snowflakes falling

Stumbling over themselves

Just to get to you

Just for the sliver of a chance

That they could maybe

Land on your little nose

Or brush the tips of your hair

In the winter

You nearly glow with heat

As the snow dusts around you

I am the opposite

In the summer

I shiver in the sun

And chill the air around me

As I wish you were here

To warm my freezing hands

ODE TO YOUR ARMS

I don't really like hugs

Too many cautionary tales

Too many nightmares

Too many bad people out there

For me to trust like I used to

This poses a problem at family events

Where I spend most of my time

Staring into space

And pretending I'm stable

After I manage to escape

The grasp of everyone in the room

When I hugged you

I almost cried

Not out of discomfort,

As I feel like doing so often with others,

I was finally home

Don't let me fall

Don't let me fall

Don't let me fall

I'll shatter like glass

Please

Just don't let me go

"Stable"

Begins with the word "stab"

Maybe

It's why I'm afraid to trust you

My back is scarred enough

When I hugged you

I almost cried

I already fell

Don't let me go

A STEP FORWARD

Some days

I wonder what you're up to

Some days

You don't even cross my mind

Maybe I'm finally moving on

BEAUTY // BEAST

They called him cruel

Heartless and hateful

Never showing mercy

They called her dainty

Delicate and small

She could break easily

When they saw him

Standing next to her

They feared for her

When they saw her

Standing next to him

They hated him

In his eyes

She saw destruction

And she loved him anyway

In her eyes

He saw salvation

And his storm never touched her

She held his heart

With gentle hands

He held her heart

Like it was his last breath

ARTIST OF SORROWS

Colors and lines and *art*
Poured out from years of
Love and heartbreak
Building and ruin

You don't know what to do
But you know that nothing feels right
Unless your hands bring life
To the lines on your canvas

Fear outlines your outlines
Doubt and worry blend into the colors
I promise that it will never go away
Fear has a way of cheating death
But no matter what you do
Please, don't let it stop your hands
Don't let the ink dry
Don't let the colors fade
Do anything but betray yourself

You are a creator,
It is in your blood

THE FUTURE – I

Today I saw the future
Well, not so much as saw than felt
But as a blind person is able
To feel someone's face and know
What they look like, I too
Felt what the future held for me
And it was more than words
Can ever tell, hard as I may try

It felt like freedom
And wearing sunglasses
At the beach on a Saturday
It felt like sitting at the table
For dinner with friends
It felt like getting an apartment
With someone who you love
With someone who loves you back
It felt like smiles and laughter
And wondering how anything
Was ever any different
And knowing that it once was
And knowing how far you've come

I still can't fully see it

But it's just around the corner

I can feel it

THE FUTURE – II

The future is coming

It's beautiful

And glorious

And *right there*

And I can't wait to meet it

OPEN LETTER TO MY HEART

An open letter to you
You know who you are
Honey dripping from your words
I was sure you'd leave by now

I was so sure I was
Hopeless
Pointless
Loveless
Lifeless

But you stop me
Speechless

You light up my life

The kindest person
The loveliest person
The most beautiful
And amazing
And wonderful
And words still fail me

Tongue tied

Tripping over myself

Smiling

Blushing

Giggling

You smile

And my heart flutters

You laugh

And my lungs falter

You simply exist

And my words fail

I wonder how you could ever

~~Like someone like me~~

Like me

Actually like me

You *actually* like *me*

~~How?~~

~~What?~~

~~Why?~~

~~Huh?~~

~~Are you sure?~~

~~Like *really* sure?~~

~~Me?~~

So many questions

But I just accept my miracle

Pretty lover
I wasn't supposed to get close to you
But rules be damned
I'm glad I did

Beautiful lover
I wasn't supposed to fall for you
But rules be damned
I'm glad I did

Gorgeous lover
I wasn't supposed to love you
But rules be damned
I'm glad I do

My lover
This is for you,
With all my heart

I love you

About the Author

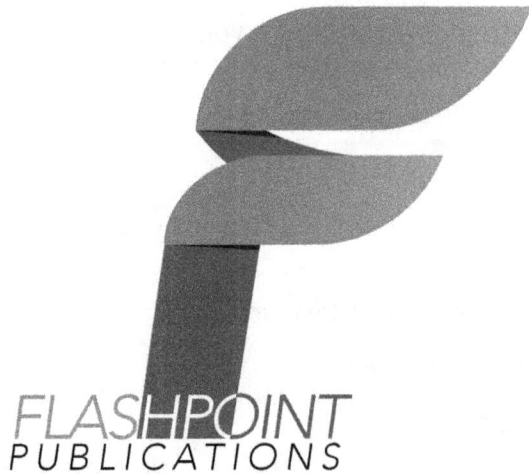

FLASHPOINT
PUBLICATIONS

Bringing Rainbow Stories to Life

Visit us at our website: www.flashpointpublications.com